Y0-AWK-872

NOV 1 7 2017

PORT WASHINGTON PUBLIC LIBRARY
ONE LIBRARY DRIVE
PORT WASHINGTON, N.Y. 11050
TEL: 883-4400

Welcome to the Desert

by Honor Head

Published in 2017 by Ruby Tuesday Books Ltd.

Copyright © 2017 Ruby Tuesday Books Ltd.

All rights reserved. No part of this publication may be reproduced in whole or in part, stored in any retrieval system, or transmitted in any form or by any means, electronic, mechanical, photocopying, recording, or otherwise, without written permission from the publisher.

Editors: Jean Coppendale and Mark J. Sachner
Designer: Emma Randall
Consultant: Sally Morgan
Production: John Lingham

Photo credits
Alamy: Cover, 12 (right), 13 (bottom), 14 (bottom), 17, 19, 21 (bottom right), 23, 24 (main), 25, 26 (main); FLPA: 10, 13 (top), 14 (top), 16, 20, 27; Getty Images: 9 (bottom); Istock Photo: 7 (top); Shutterstock: Cover, 3, 4–5, 6, 7 (bottom), 8, 9 (top), 12 (left), 15, 18, 21 (top), 21 (bottom left), 22, 24 (right), 26 (right), 28, 29 (bottom), 30-31; Superstock: 11, 29 (top).

Library of Congress Control Number: 2017908522

Print ISBN: 978-1-911341-93-2
eBook ISBN: 978-1-911341-94-9

Printed and published in the United States of America

For further information including rights and permissions requests, please contact our Customer Service Department at 877-337-8577.

Contents

Welcome to the Desert 4

Spring in the Desert 6

Spiny Survivors 8

A Nest in a Saguaro Cactus 10

Watch Out! 12

Keeping Cool 14

A Busy Night 16

Eat It Clean! 18

Minibeast Feast 20

Desert Hide and Seek 22

Rain, Glorious Rain! 24

Big Cats of the Desert 26

Winter in the Desert 28

A Desert Food Web 30

Glossary 31

Index, Read More, Learn More Online 32

Words shown in **bold** in the text are explained in the glossary.

Welcome to the Desert

Who and what lives in the Sonoran Desert in the United States?

This hot, dry, dusty desert is home to spiky cacti and other plants.

Birds, snakes, lizards, and wild cats are some of the animals that live in this **habitat**.

The plants and animals get what they need to live from the desert.

A desert is a type of ecosystem. An ecosystem includes all the living things in an area. It also includes non-living things, such as sand, rocks, sun, and rain. Everything in an ecosystem has its own part to play.

Let's find out what happens in this habitat. Welcome to the desert!

Spring in the Desert

It is spring in the Sonoran Desert.

Colorful flowers provide food for insects, birds, and other animals.

Cacti also help animals in the Sonoran Desert survive in lots of ways.

Cactus

Queen butterfly

Ground squirrel

A tiny ground squirrel nibbles on a cactus flower.

Butterflies and birds drink **nectar** from cactus flowers.

Gila woodpecker

In spring and summer, the Sonoran Desert is scorching hot during the day. There may be no rain for many months.

Cactus flower

How do cacti survive in the hot, dry desert?

Spiny Survivors

Cacti have **adapted** to survive in a dry desert habitat.

When it rains, a cactus's roots quickly take up lots of water.

The soft, fleshy plant expands to hold as much water as possible.

Saguaro cactus

The plant's fat stems are full of water.

Some cacti have a long, thick taproot that grows deep into the ground to find water. Thinner roots spread out near the surface to quickly suck up water when it rains.

Eating the juicy stems of a cactus is a good way for animals to get water.

The plant's spines help protect its stems from hungry, thirsty animals.

A prickly pear cactus

Spines

Fruit

These fat pads are the plant's stems.

Fruit

Javelina

Barrel cactus

This javelina is carefully eating fruit from a spiky barrel cactus.

What lives inside a hole in a saguaro cactus?

A Nest in a Saguaro Cactus

A Gila woodpecker is pecking a hole in a saguaro cactus.

The hole is a cool, safe nest where she can lay her eggs.

The woodpecker pecks away rotting, diseased bits of stem.

This helps the cactus by stopping the disease from spreading to the rest of the plant.

Gila woodpecker

Baby elf owl

An elf owl is the size of a coffee mug. She doesn't make her own nest hole. She raises her chicks in a hole that a woodpecker family no longer uses.

Hawk

Chick

A hawk has made a nest of sticks in a cactus.

High above the ground, her chicks will be safe from snakes and other **predators**.

What food does the hawk catch for her hungry chicks?

Watch Out!

Hawk

The hawk flies high in the sky looking for food for her chicks.

She has excellent eyesight and can spot small animals on the ground.

Ground squirrels

A family of ground squirrels is outside their **burrow**.

The ground squirrels are eating grass, leaves, flowers, fruit, and seeds.

In the desert there is very little water. Ground squirrels get the water they need from the plants they eat.

Suddenly, the mother ground squirrel sees the hawk overhead.

The squirrel family dives to safety in their underground burrow.

A ground squirrel peeks out of its burrow.

Can you think of another reason why a desert animal might spend time in a burrow?

Keeping Cool

It's midday, and the scorching sun beats down on the desert.

Many animals are underground, where it is cool.

Desert tortoise

Prickly pear fruit

Desert tortoises dig burrows in the rocky soil.

When evening comes, a desert tortoise leaves its burrow to find plants to eat.

A Gila monster lizard stays cool in an old desert tortoise burrow.

A rattlesnake sleeps in the shade under some rocks.

When the air cools down, it goes hunting.

Gila monster

Rattlesnake

The rattlesnake hunts for small animals, such as rats and ground squirrels. It injects **venom** into its **prey** through its fangs, and then swallows its prey whole.

What happens in the desert when darkness falls?

A Busy Night

When night falls, **nocturnal** animals leave their homes to find food.

A long-nosed bat flies from its home in a cool, rocky cave.

It visits cacti and other plants to drink nectar from flowers.

As the bat feeds, **pollen** sticks to its furry face.

It carries the pollen from flower to flower, which helps the plants make seeds.

Long-nosed bat

The bat uses its tongue like a straw to sip up nectar.

Burrow

Kangaroo rat

Pouch filled with seeds

A kangaroo rat hops about, looking for seeds. It carries food back to its burrow in its cheek pouches.

A long howl fills the night air. What is making that noise?

17

Eat It Clean!

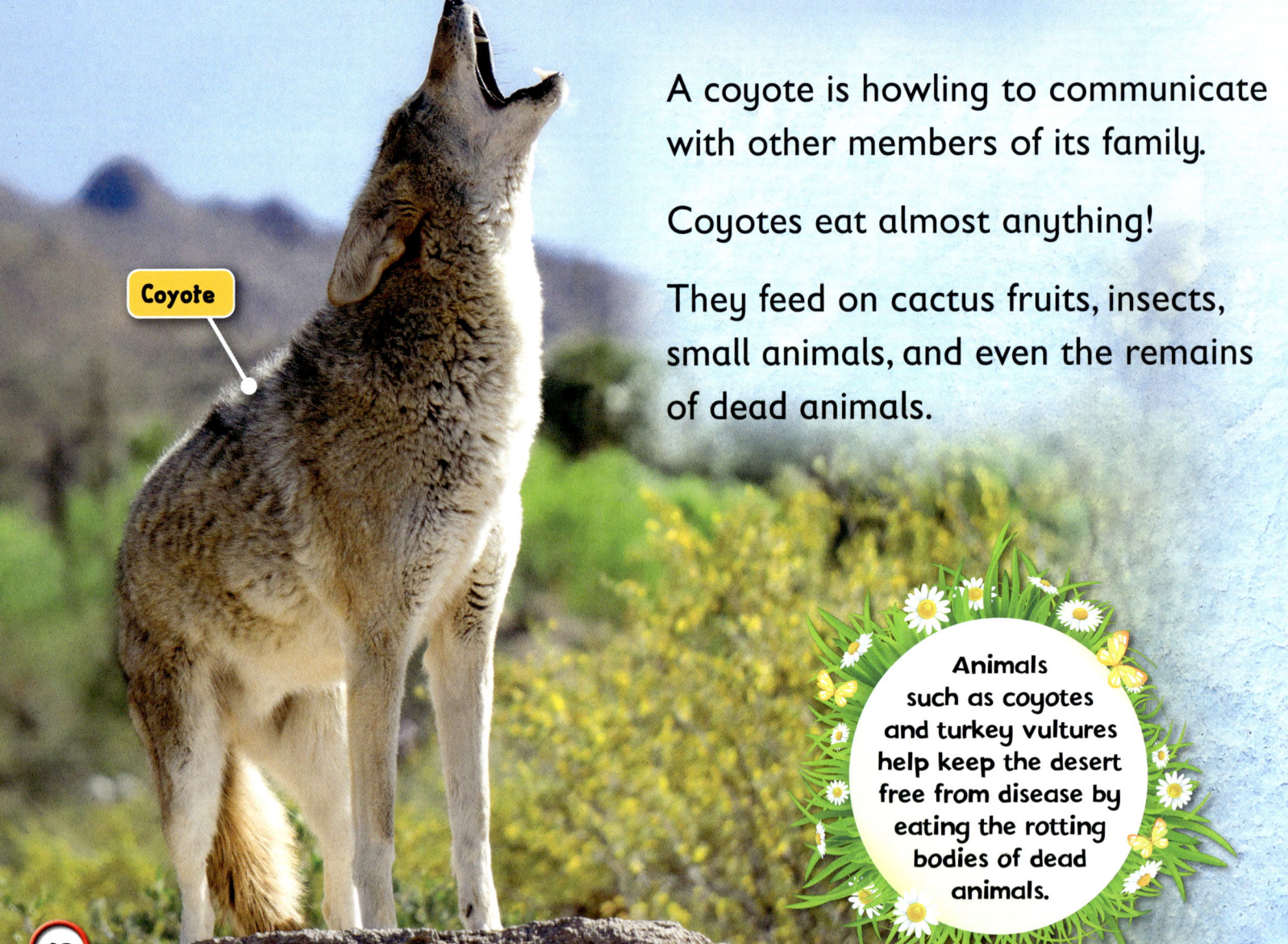

Coyote

A coyote is howling to communicate with other members of its family.

Coyotes eat almost anything!

They feed on cactus fruits, insects, small animals, and even the remains of dead animals.

Animals such as coyotes and turkey vultures help keep the desert free from disease by eating the rotting bodies of dead animals.

This turkey vulture is eating the remains of an old javelina.

Beetles, such as the stinkbug, also feed on dead bodies and rotting plants.

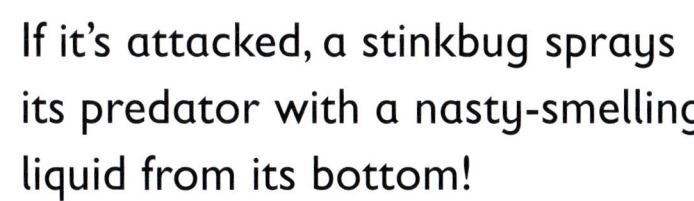

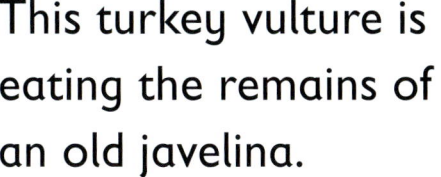

If it's attacked, a stinkbug sprays its predator with a nasty-smelling liquid from its bottom!

Which clever hunter has built a trap underground?

Minibeast Feast

Trapdoor

Under a trapdoor in the ground waits a tiny, eight-legged predator.

Trapdoor spider

When an insect walks near the door, the ground **vibrates**.

The trapdoor spider feels the vibrations and jumps out to grab its meal.

A scorpion grabs small animals in its pincers. It uses the venomous sting at the end of its tail to stop its prey from struggling.

A tarantula spider waits in its burrow.

Silk threads outside the burrow vibrate when an insect walks by.

Then the tarantula jumps out and bites its prey.

How does an animal's color help it survive in the desert?

Desert Hide and Seek

Some desert animals have **camouflage** to help them survive.

Camouflage is the colors or markings that help an animal blend in with its habitat.

The skin color of a regal horned lizard helps it hide from predators on the rocky ground.

Many desert animals are a sandy color.

Baby javelinas are camouflaged to keep them safe from hunters, such as coyotes.

Can you spot a coyote?

A coyote's color helps it hide from its prey when it is hunting.

What does it mean when the air grows cooler and a breeze blows over the desert?

Rain, Glorious Rain!

Lightning flashes over the desert.

The **monsoon** rains have come.

Spadefoot toad

After the rains, spadefoot toads leave their underground burrows to **mate** and lay eggs in puddles and pools.

In less than a day, tadpoles hatch from the eggs.

The tadpoles change into toads in just two weeks, before the puddles dry out.

Then each tiny toad buries itself in the sand until the next rains.

Toad tadpole

Before going underground, the young toads feed on ants, beetles, grasshoppers, and spiders. It may be a year before they eat their next meal!

What powerful predator lives in the mountains that tower over the desert?

25

Big Cats of the Desert

The mountains of the Sonoran Desert are home to mountain lions.

Mountain lion

They hunt large animals, such as deer, bighorn sheep, and javelinas.

Mountain lions are also known as pumas or cougars. They can leap up to 40 feet (12 m) in one jump.

Bighorn sheep

Mountain lion cubs have spotted coats so they are camouflaged in their den.

Their spots help hide them from coyotes when their mother is out hunting.

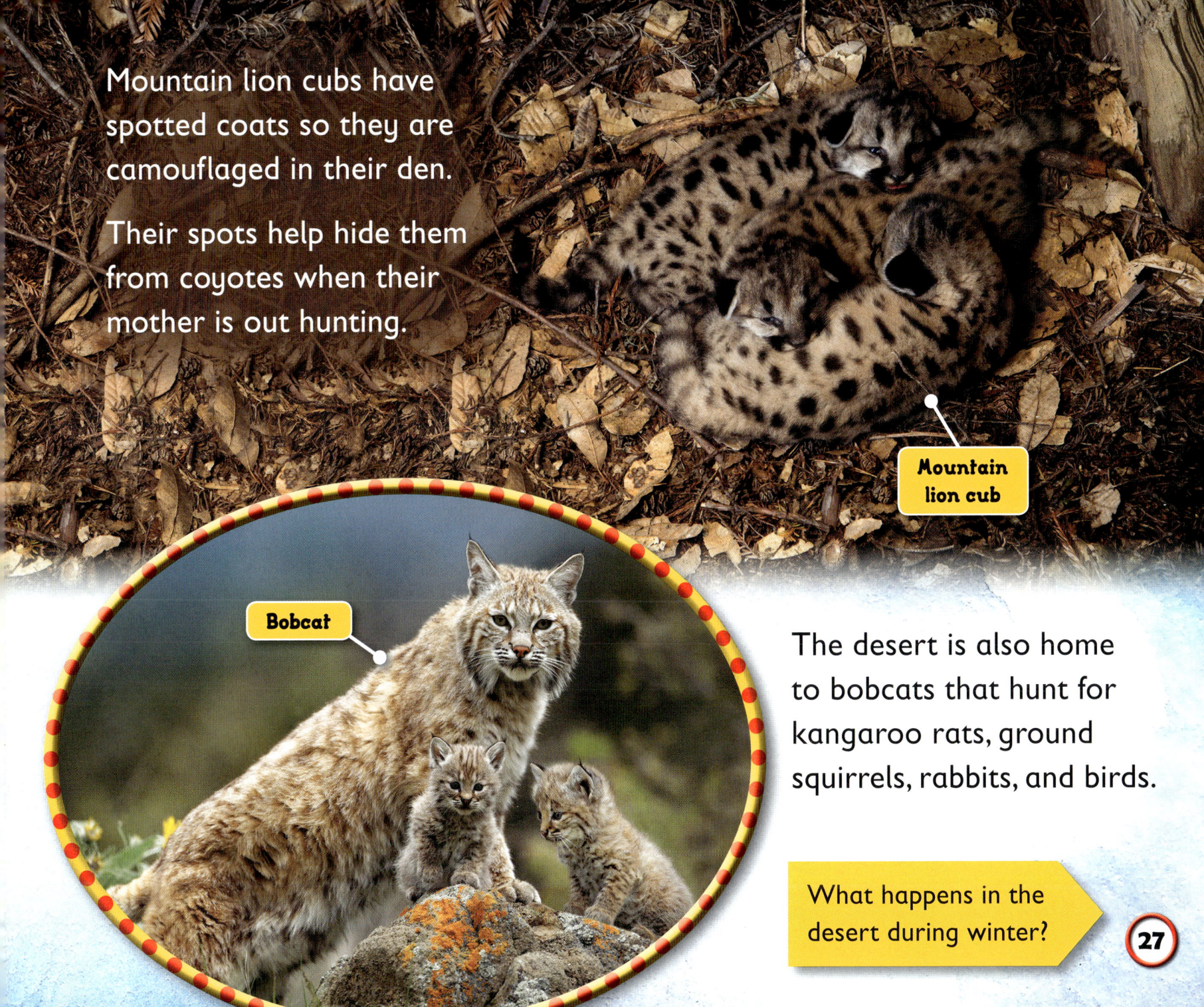

Mountain lion cub

Bobcat

The desert is also home to bobcats that hunt for kangaroo rats, ground squirrels, rabbits, and birds.

What happens in the desert during winter?

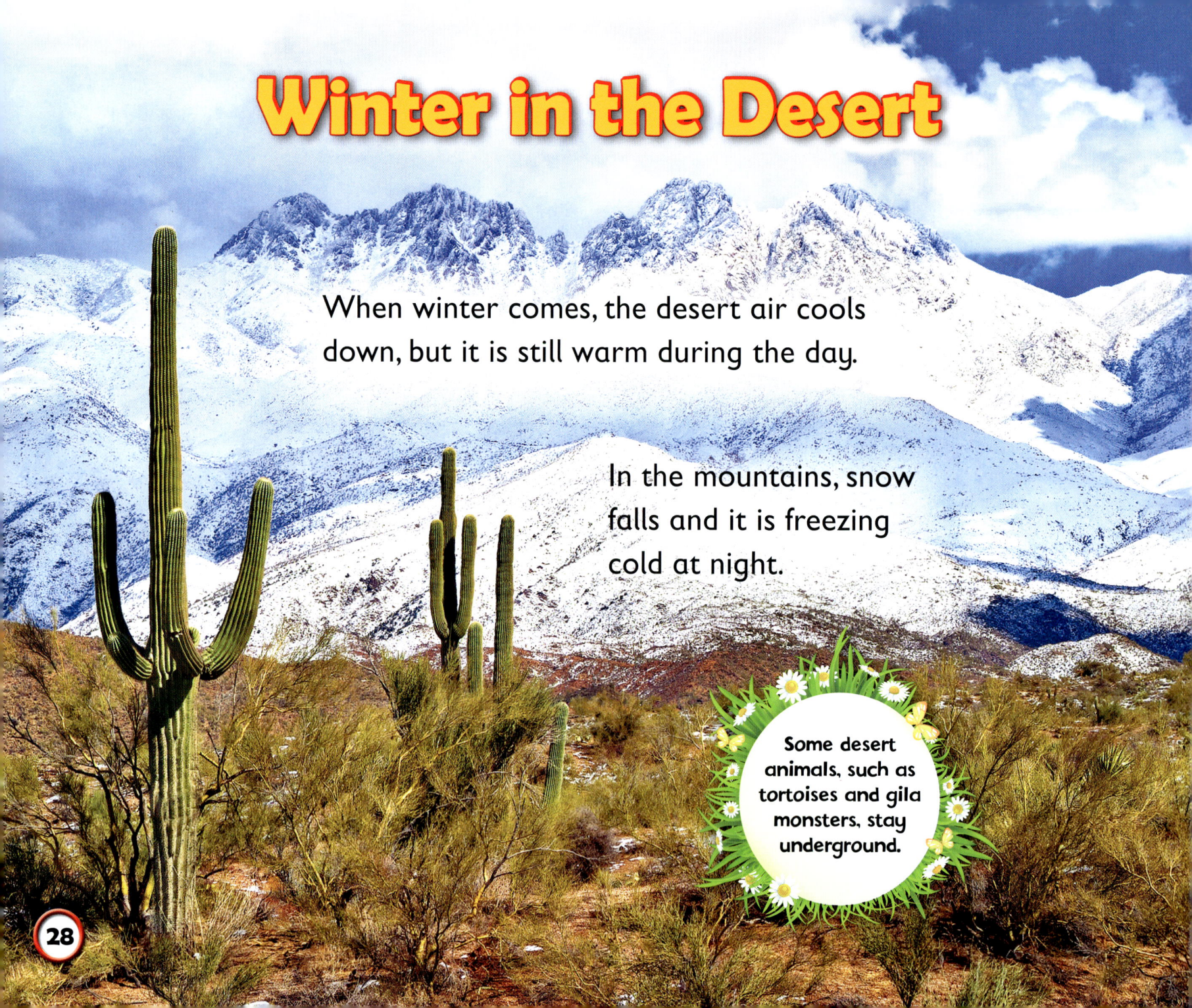

Winter in the Desert

When winter comes, the desert air cools down, but it is still warm during the day.

In the mountains, snow falls and it is freezing cold at night.

Some desert animals, such as tortoises and gila monsters, stay underground.

In the cooler weather, birds build nests and mate.

A tiny hummingbird builds a nest of twigs, leaves, and spider webs.

Hummingbird

Dove

A dove finds a spot in a cactus for her nest.

Winter in the desert is short. The hot days of spring and summer will soon be back.

A Desert Food Web

A food web shows who eats who in a habitat.

This food web shows the connections between some of the living things in the Sonoran Desert.

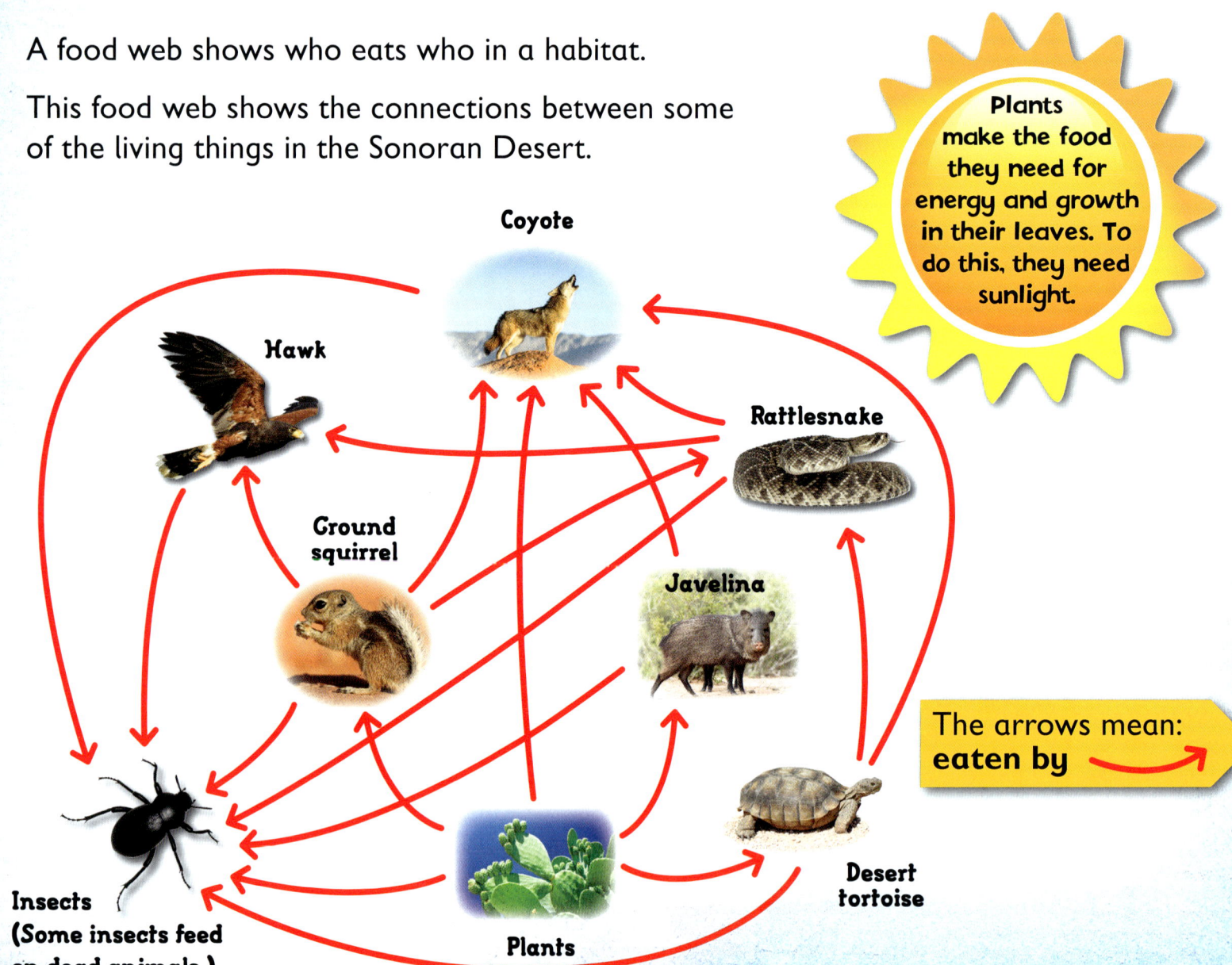

Plants make the food they need for energy and growth in their leaves. To do this, they need sunlight.

The arrows mean: **eaten by**

Glossary

adapted (uh-DAP-tid)
Changed over time to survive in a particular habitat.

burrow (BUR-oh)
A hole or tunnel that an animal digs as a home.

camouflage (KAM-uh-flahzh)
Colors or markings that help an animal blend into its habitat.

habitat (HAB-uh-tat)
The place where an animal or plant lives. Deserts, rain forests, and backyards are all types of habitats.

mate (MATE)
To get together to produce young.

monsoon (mahn-SOON)
Very heavy rains that happen at least once a year.

nectar (NEK-tur)
A sugary liquid produced by flowers.

nocturnal (nok-TUR-nuhl)
Active mainly at night.

pollen (POL-uhn)
A colored dust that is made by flowers, and is needed for making seeds.

predator (PRED-uh-tur)
An animal that hunts and eats other animals.

prey (PRAY)
An animal that is hunted by other animals for food.

venom (VEN-uhm)
A type of poison that is injected into a body by a bite or sting.

vibrate (VYE-brate)
To move very quickly backward and forward.

Index

B
bats 16
birds 4, 6–7, 10–11, 12–13, 18–19, 27, 29, 30
bobcats 4, 27
burrows 12–13, 14–15, 17, 21, 24–25, 28

C
cacti 4, 6–7, 8–9, 10–11, 14, 16, 18, 29, 30
camouflage 22–23, 27
coyotes 18, 23, 27, 30

F
flowers 6–7, 9, 13, 16
fruit 9, 13, 14, 18

G
Gila monsters 5, 15, 28
Gila woodpeckers 7, 10–11
ground squirrels 7, 12–13, 15, 27, 30

H
hawks 11, 12–13, 30

I
insects 6–7, 18–19, 20–21, 25, 30

J
javelinas 9, 19, 23, 26, 30

K
kangaroo rats 16, 27

L
lizards 4–5, 15, 22, 28

M
mountain lions 26–27

N
nests 10–11, 29

P
predators 11, 12–13, 15, 18–19, 20–21, 22–23, 25, 26–27, 30
prey 12–13, 15, 18–19, 20–21, 22–23, 25, 26–27, 30

R
rains 5, 7, 8, 24–25

S
scorpions 21
seeds 13, 16–17
snakes 4, 11, 15, 30
spiders 20–21, 25, 29

T
tadpoles 25
toads 24–25
tortoises 14–15, 28, 30

Read More

Owen, Ruth. *Let's Investigate Habitats and Food Chains (Get Started With STEM).* New York: Ruby Tuesday Books (2017).

Phillips, Dee. *Desert Tortoise's Burrow (The Hole Truth: Animal Life Underground).* New York: Bearport Publishing (2015).

Learn More Online

To learn more about life in a desert, go to
www.rubytuesdaybooks.com/habitats